Neptune

ELAINE LANDAU

Children's Press®
A Division of Scholastic Inc.
New York Toronto London Auckland Sydney
Mexico City New Delhi Hong Kong
Danbury, Connecticut

Content Consultant

Michelle Yehling

Astronomy Education Consultant

Aurora, Illinois

Reading Consultant

Cecilia Minden-Cupp, PhD

Early Literacy Consultant and Author

Library of Congress Cataloging-in-Publication Data

Landau, Elaine.
  Neptune / by Elaine Landau.
    p. cm. — (A true book)
  Includes bibliographical references and index.
   ISBN-13: 978-0-531-12563-2 (lib. bdg.)   978-0-531-14793-1 (pbk.)
   ISBN-10: 0-531-12563-7 (lib. bdg.)   0-531-14793-2 (pbk.)
  1. Neptune (Planet)—Juvenile literature. I. Title. II. Series.
  QB691.L36 2008
  523.48'1—dc22   2007008257

All rights reserved. Published in 2008 by Children's Press, an imprint of Scholastic Inc.
Published simultaneously in Canada. Printed in the United States of America.
SCHOLASTIC, CHILDREN'S PRESS, A TRUE BOOK, and associated logos are trademarks and/or registered trademarks of Scholastic Inc.
1 2 3 4 5 6 7 8 9 10 R 17 16 15 14 13 12 11 10 09

Find the Truth!

Everything you are about to read is true *except* for one of the sentences on this page.

Which one is **TRUE**?

T or F   The temperature in Neptune's core is colder than the temperature on the surface of the sun.

T or F   Neptune is the farthest planet from the sun.

Find the answer in this book.

Contents

1 A Trip to Neptune

How long would it take to get there?
Why would anyone want to go?. **7**

2 Neptune in the Solar System

How long is a year on Neptune?. **13**

THE BIG TRUTH!

Which Planet Is Farthest from the Sun?

Is the answer as simple
as you think?. **20**

3 Discovering Neptune

How did astronomers find it? **22**

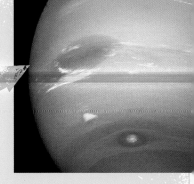

If you weighed 100 pounds on Earth, you would weigh 110 pounds on Neptune.

4 All about Neptune

What's below the stormy blue clouds?....... **27**

5 Moons and Rings

What's so special about Neptune's rings? **33**

6 Missions to Neptune

Has any spaceship made it that far? **39**

True Statistics **43**
Resources **44**
Important Words **46**
Index **47**
About the Author **48**

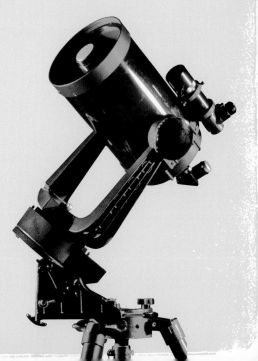

An artist created this image of the *Voyager 2* spacecraft reaching Neptune. From Neptune, the sun would look like a bright star.

CHAPTER 1

A Trip to Neptune

It would take a spacecraft about 10 years to travel to Neptune.

Which planet is farthest from the sun? If you answered Neptune, you're correct! Neptune is about 3 billion miles (5 billion kilometers) from the sun. That's 30 times the distance between Earth and the sun. No human being has ever traveled that far.

Neptune's blue clouds are hundreds of degrees colder than the coldest temperature ever recorded on Earth.

Imagine that you could travel to Neptune in a spaceship. As you got farther from Earth, our planet would look smaller and smaller. The sun would also begin to look smaller as you flew toward Neptune.

You might pass other planets in the **solar system**. The solar system is made up of the sun and all the planets that travel around it. The solar system contains other objects, too, such as icy **comets** and rocky **asteroids**. On the way to Neptune, you might pass Mars, Jupiter, Saturn, and Uranus. You might even get close to a **dwarf planet** known as Pluto.

Most asteroids have craters from crashing into other space objects.

This drawing shows a scene you might see on your way to Neptune. You could spot the planet Uranus and many space rocks called asteroids.

After about 10 years, you would get close to Neptune. You would see a big, blue planet covered in swirling clouds. You might also catch a glimpse of Neptune's faint rings or spot one of its moons.

You could not land your spaceship on Neptune, however. There is no hard surface to land on. This is because Neptune is made mostly of liquid and gas.

A space probe took this photo of Neptune's clouds. Under the clouds are more gases and liquid.

How Neptune Got Its Name

The ancient Romans named the five planets they could see in the sky—Mercury, Venus, Mars, Jupiter, and Saturn. They named the planets after their gods. But Neptune was not discovered until 1846. It was found by **astronomers**. Some people wanted to name it Leverrier (luh-ver-YAY), after a man who helped discover it.

After much discussion, astronomers agreed to call the planet Neptune. Neptune is the ancient Roman god of the sea. This new blue planet reminded astronomers of Earth's oceans.

The god Neptune was said to live in a palace on the ocean floor and drown sailors with fierce storms.

11

You might spot Neptune through a telescope such as this. The planet would look like a small blue circle.

CHAPTER 2

Neptune in the Solar System

Neptune is the only planet in the solar system that you can't see from Earth without a telescope.

In 2006, Neptune got a new place in the solar system. For many years, Pluto was considered the most distant planet. Now Neptune is the most distant. How did that happen?

An artist created this illustration of Neptune and its rings.

13

Neptune didn't move farther from the sun. Instead, Pluto got a new title. It used to be called a planet. Now astronomers say it's a dwarf planet.

There are seven planets closer to the sun than Neptune—Mercury, Venus, Earth, Mars, Jupiter, Saturn, and Uranus. The planets and other objects in the solar system **orbit**, or travel around, the sun.

Our solar system has at least 162 moons. Moons orbit planets. Some planets have many moons. Neptune has 13!

This illustration shows Jupiter and two of its largest moons.

Jupiter has at least 63 moons.

Io

Europa

Neptune's Travels

The sun is a huge ball of bubbling hot gas.

All the planets stay in their orbits because of **gravity**. Gravity is the force that pulls objects toward each other. The massive sun has a huge amount of gravity. The sun's gravity pulls on the planets. This force keeps the planets from flying out into space.

The amount of time it takes a planet to travel around the sun once equals one year on that planet. Earth orbits the sun in about 365 days, so that is the length of an Earth year. Earth is closer to the sun than Neptune, however. So Neptune has to travel farther to go around the sun. It takes Neptune 165 Earth years to orbit the sun. You would not want to wait for your birthday to come on that faraway planet!

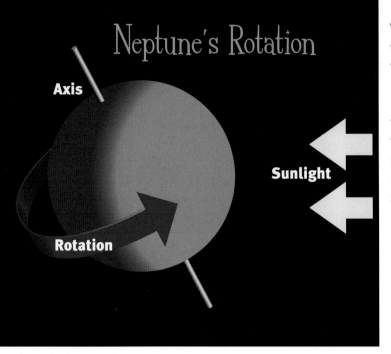

Neptune's Rotation

Axis

Sunlight

Rotation

The red arrow in this diagram shows the direction of Neptune's rotation. It is daytime on the side that faces the sun. As the planet rotates, new parts move into the sunlight.

Spinning Around

As Neptune orbits the sun, it also rotates, or spins, on its **axis**. An axis is an imaginary line that runs from north to south through the center of a planet.

The time it takes a planet to rotate once on its axis equals one day on that planet. A day on Earth is about 24 hours long. Neptune spins quickly on its axis, however. A day on Neptune is about 16 Earth hours long.

How Big Is Big?

Neptune is called a gas giant. Gas giants are huge planets made mostly of liquid and gas. Saturn, Uranus, and Jupiter are also gas giants.

Neptune is the smallest gas giant.

This diagram shows the size of Neptune compared to the size of Earth.

Earth

Neptune

Neptune's Solar System

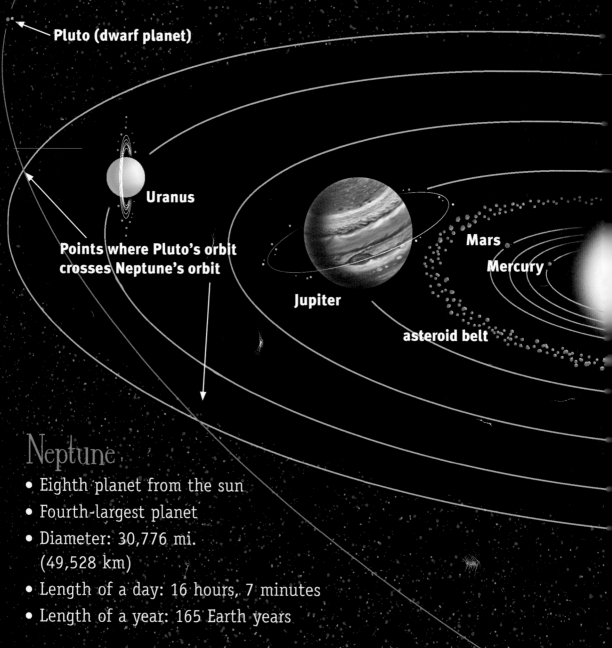

Pluto (dwarf planet)

Uranus

Points where Pluto's orbit crosses Neptune's orbit

Jupiter

Mars

Mercury

asteroid belt

Neptune

- Eighth planet from the sun
- Fourth-largest planet
- Diameter: 30,776 mi. (49,528 km)
- Length of a day: 16 hours, 7 minutes
- Length of a year: 165 Earth years

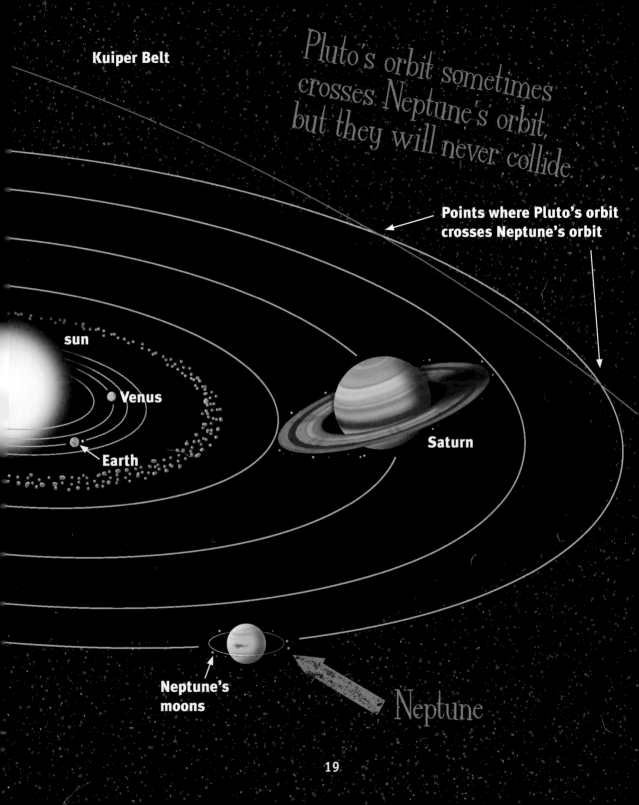

Kuiper Belt

Pluto's orbit sometimes crosses Neptune's orbit, but they will never collide.

Points where Pluto's orbit crosses Neptune's orbit

sun

Venus

Earth

Saturn

Neptune's moons

Neptune

1846 : Neptune

Astronomer Johann Galle finds Neptune.

1930 : Pluto

American astronomer Clyde Tombaugh discovers Pluto.

1979 : Neptune

Pluto's strange orbit brings it inside Neptune's orbit. Neptune is now the outermost planet.

1999 : Pluto

Pluto crosses Neptune's orbit again and becomes the outermost planet.

2006 : Neptune

Astronomers decide that Pluto is a dwarf planet. Once again, Neptune is the eighth and most distant planet.

Which Planet Is Farthest from the Sun?

How would you answer this question to get an A on your science test? It depends on the year in which you take the test!

1543 : Saturn

Polish astronomer Nicolaus Copernicus publishes a book with a picture that becomes famous—one of the first models of the solar system. The sun is in the center. Saturn is the sixth and most distant planet.

1781 : Uranus

British astronomer Sir William Herschel discovers Uranus beyond Saturn.

CHAPTER 3

Discovering Neptune

Neptune is about 2.7 billion miles from Earth.

You can't see Neptune without a telescope. The planet is too far away. The other planets in the solar system can be seen with the human eye. How did astronomers discover Neptune if they couldn't see it?

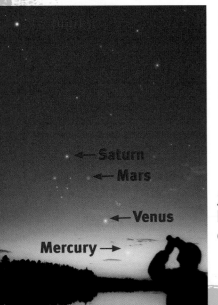

Saturn
Mars
Venus
Mercury

Jupiter, Saturn, Mars, Venus, and Mercury can be seen in the night sky. Once in a while you can see them all together.

22

Something pulls at the planet Uranus as it orbits the sun. It makes Uranus wobble slightly.

It all started with Uranus. Uranus is the seventh planet from the sun. Uranus is Neptune's neighbor. It was discovered in 1781. That was 65 years before anyone saw Neptune.

Astronomers noticed that Uranus was not orbiting the sun the way it should. Something was making it wobble. Astronomers wondered if gravity from another planet could be pulling on Uranus.

John C. Adams　　　　**Urbain Leverrier**

Astronomers once called
Neptune "Leverrier's Planet."

Two people worked separately to figure out
a location for this possible new planet. One was
John C. Adams, an English astronomer. The other
was French **mathematician** Urbain Leverrier (luh-
ver-YAY). They didn't try to find the mystery planet
using telescopes. They tried to find it using math.

What kind of object could make Uranus wobble as it did? Where could that object be? Both men figured out that there must be a large planet about a billion miles beyond Uranus.

No one ever checked Adams's math with a telescope. But Leverrier sent his findings to German astronomer Johann Galle, in 1846. Galle pointed his telescope to where Leverrier said a planet would be. Leverrier was right! Galle found a tiny blue dot in the sky. A new planet, Neptune, had been discovered.

In 1612, the astronomer Galileo spotted Neptune with his telescope. He thought it was a star, not a planet!

Galileo studied the night sky through a telescope.

This photo taken by the Hubble Space Telescope shows Neptune and four of its moons. Neptune has at least 13 moons.

CHAPTER 4

All about Neptune

Astronomers have measured stronger winds on Neptune than on any other planet in the solar system.

Neptune and Earth are both planets orbiting the sun. Neptune is a lot different from Earth, though. Neptune is huge. It is made mostly of liquids, gases, ice, and rock. Swirling blue clouds race across the planet at tremendous speeds.

This photograph of Earth was taken on December 7, 1972, from *Apollo 17*.

What Is Neptune Made Of?

Neptune's outer layer is mostly made up of the gases helium (HEE-lee-uhm), hydrogen (HY-druh-juhn), and methane (ME-thane). These gases form Neptune's **atmosphere**. An atmosphere is the blanket of gases that surrounds a planet or a moon. Neptune's atmosphere is full of thick clouds.

Neptune's atmosphere gives the planet its color. When sunlight hits methane gas, it looks blue.

This drawing shows what Neptune might look like if a section were cut out.

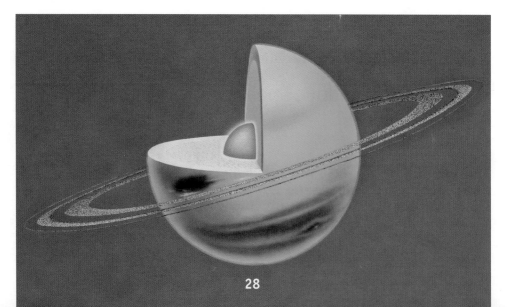

The Pressure Is On

Neptune's thick atmosphere presses down on the liquids and gases that make up the planet. The deeper you go into the planet, the greater the pressure. Astronomers think this pressure turns the gas in the planet to liquid.

Astronomers know that the liquids of Neptune are very hot. They are about 8,500 degrees Fahrenheit (4,700 degrees Celsius). No one knows for sure why they are so hot.

The core, or center, of Neptune is an even bigger mystery. Astronomers think the core might be a huge ball of melted rock and metal. Neptune's core might be as hot as 10,000°F (5,500°C)!

← The temperature in Neptune's core is as hot as the surface of the sun!

How's the Weather on Neptune?

The inside of Neptune is blazing hot, but little heat from the core reaches the clouds. Not much of the sun's heat reaches Neptune, either. This means the cloudy outer layer is very cold. The temperatures there drop as low as −353°F (−214°C)!

Neptune has strong winds and huge storms. The winds in Neptune's atmosphere can blow at speeds of more than 1,200 miles (1,930 km) per hour. That is about 10 times more powerful than the strongest hurricane on Earth!

The Great Dark Spot:
Now You See It, Now You Don't

In 1989, astronomers spotted a huge, oval-shaped storm on Neptune. This storm was spinning like a hurricane. It was as big as Earth! They named the storm the Great Dark Spot.

Astronomers think the dark center of the storm was a huge hole in the atmosphere of Neptune. The winds around the hole blew as fast as 700 miles (1,100 km) per hour.

In 1994, astronomers looked for the Great Dark Spot again. It was gone! Astronomers are not sure why it disappeared.

Great Dark Spot

Neptune

This photograph taken by the Voyager 2 spacecraft shows Neptune with its largest moon, Triton.

Triton

CHAPTER 5

Moons and Rings

One of Neptune's moons is named Despina. In Greek mythology, Despina was Neptune's daughter.

Neptune has 13 known moons. They are made of rock and ice. Five of the moons are tiny and have irregular shapes. Astronomers think they are pieces of a larger moon that exploded when a comet crashed into it.

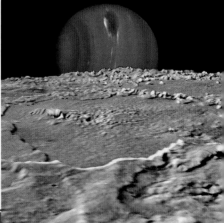

This is a view of Neptune from the surface of Triton, one of its moons. Triton's surface has been compared to the skin of a cantaloupe.

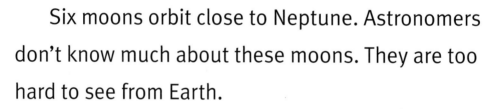

A moon called Nereid (foreground) has a strange orbit. At times, it is millions of miles closer to Neptune than at other times. The distance between this moon and Neptune can vary by more than 5 million miles (8 million km).

Six moons orbit close to Neptune. Astronomers don't know much about these moons. They are too hard to see from Earth.

Triton and Nereid (NEE-reed) are two of Neptune's largest moons. Astronomers think they used to be asteroids that were grabbed by Neptune's gravity. They started to orbit Neptune. Nereid is the farthest moon from Neptune.

A Unique Moon

Triton is an unusual moon. It may be the coldest place in the solar system. Its temperature can drop as low as −391°F (−235°C). Even Triton's volcanoes are made of ice. They are called ice volcanoes.

Triton's ice volcanoes shoot a mixture of gases and dust into the atmosphere. The mixture freezes instantly and falls down as snow. Some volcanoes shoot their icy mixture 6 miles (10 km) high.

Triton is unusal in another way. The moon is slowly sinking closer to Neptune. Neptune's gravity will someday pull Triton too close to the planet. Then the moon will break into many pieces.

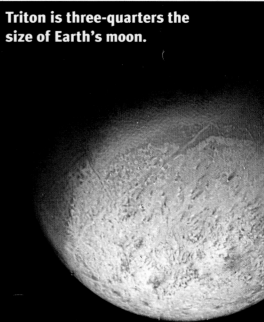

Triton is three-quarters the size of Earth's moon.

This illustration shows the rings around each of the gas giants.

Jupiter, Uranus, Saturn, and Neptune all have rings.

Neptune's Rings

Neptune has at least six rings. They are not as colorful or as beautiful as Saturn's rings, however. Astronomers think Neptune's rings are made up of tiny pieces of dark dust. The dark material makes them hard to see from Earth, even with the help of a telescope.

Some parts of Neptune's rings are so thin that they are almost invisible. Other parts are very thick. Astronomers think this is because of the gravity from Neptune's moons. The gravity causes the dust in the rings to clump together.

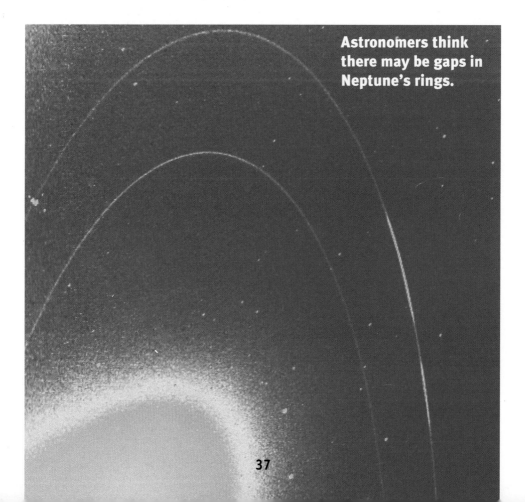

Astronomers think there may be gaps in Neptune's rings.

Voyager 2 was packaged inside a cone. Giant rockets launched it into space. After reaching Neptune in 1989, *Voyager 2* continued to travel toward the outer edge of the solar system.

CHAPTER 6

Missions to Neptune

As of 2006, Voyager 2 was about 7.4 billion miles from Earth.

No human has traveled to Neptune because it is so far away. How can scientists learn about this distant planet? One of the best ways is to send spaceships without people inside them. These spaceships are called **space probes**.

Voyager 2 **reached Jupiter in 1979, Saturn in 1981, Uranus in 1986, and Neptune in 1989.**

So far, only one space probe has traveled to Neptune. *Voyager 2* was launched into space in 1977. It flew by Jupiter, Saturn, and Uranus before reaching Neptune on August 25, 1989.

Voyager 2 flew within 3,000 miles (4,830 km) of Neptune. That's less than the distance between New York City and Los Angeles! The space probe also flew by Triton. We can thank *Voyager 2* for most of what we know about Neptune and Triton. The space probe photographed Neptune for five months. It measured the planet's temperature. *Voyager 2* discovered six more moons and took pictures of Triton's ice volcanoes.

Just in case aliens find Voyager 2, the space probe is carrying a recording with greetings in 55 languages.

After flying by Neptune and Triton, *Voyager 2* continued its journey into space. The probe is now twice as far away from the sun as Pluto is. Eventually, it will leave our solar system.

This drawing shows *Voyager 2* passing Neptune. The spacecraft will send information from space until it runs out of power in around 2020.

There is a lot more to learn about Neptune. Astronomers know almost nothing about the layers beneath Neptune's clouds, for example. They are not sure why storms appear and disappear.

A space probe called *Neptune/Triton Orbiter* might launch in 2035. That probe could answer some of the questions astronomers have about

Neptune. Until then, astronomers will do the best they can to study Neptune with telescopes. ★

An artist created this image of *Orbiter* (top), two of its probes, Neptune (background), and Triton.

42

True Statistics

Classification: Gas giant

Year discovered: 1846

Named after: Roman god of the sea

Number of moons: 13

Number of rings: At least 4

Atmosphere: Yes

Atmospheric temperature: About −353°F (−214°C)

Distance from the sun: About 2.8 billion mi. (4.5 billion km)

Distance from Earth: About 2.7 billion mi. (4.3 billion km)

Length of a day: About 16 Earth hours

Length of a year: 165 Earth years

Did you find the truth?

(F) The temperature in Neptune's core is colder than the temperature on the surface of the sun.

(T) Neptune is the farthest planet from the sun.

Resources

Books

Chrismer, Melanie. *Neptune*. New York, NY: Children's Press, 2007.

Hansen, Ole Steen. *Space Flights*. New York: Crabtree, 2004.

Kerrod, Robin. *Space Probes*. Milwaukee, WI: World Almanac Library, 2005.

Somervill, Barbara A. *The History of Space Travel*. Chanhassen, MN: The Child's World, 2004.

Vogt, Gregory. *Comets*. Mankato, MN: Bridgestone Books, 2002.

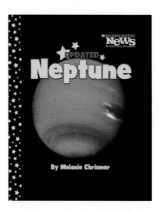

Organizations and Web Sites

Astronomy for Kids — Neptune

www.kidsastronomy.com/neptune.htm

Check out this site for more on Neptune and the other planets.

Voyager: The Interstellar Mission

voyager.jpl.nasa.gov/

Read all about *Voyager's* mission to the outer planets and beyond.

National Space Society

www.nss.org

1620 I Street NW, Suite 615

Washington, DC 20006

202-429-1600

This organization works toward humans successfully living and working in space.

Places to Visit

Kennedy Space Center

Kennedy Space Center, FL 32899

www.ksc.nasa.gov

Explore NASA's launch headquarters and learn more about some of the organization's space missions.

Smithsonian National Air and Space Museum

Independence Avenue at 4th Street, SW

Washington, DC 20560

202-633-1000

www.nasm.si.edu

Important Words

asteroids (AS-tuh-roidz) – large pieces of rock that orbit the sun

astronomers (uh-STRAW-nuh-murz) – scientists who study the planets, stars, and space

atmosphere (AT-mu-sfihr) – the blanket of gases that surrounds a planet or a moon

axis (AK-siss) – an imaginary line that runs through the center of a planet or other object

comets – large chunks of rock and ice that travel around the sun

dwarf planet – a body in the solar system that orbits the sun, has a constant (nearly round) shape, is not a moon, and has an orbit that overlaps with the orbits of other bodies

gravity – a force that pulls two objects together; gravity pulls you down onto Earth

mathematician – a person who specializes in mathematics

orbit – to travel around an object such as a sun or planet

solar system (SOH-lur SISS-tuhm) – a sun and all the objects that travel around it

space probes – spaceships that travel without astronauts on board

Index

Adams, John C., **24**, 25
asteroids, 8, **9**, **18–19**, 34
astronomers, 11, 14, 21, 22, 23, **24**, 25, 27, 29, 31, 33, 34, 36, 37, 42
atmosphere, 28, 29, 30, **31**, 35
axis, **16**

clouds, **7**, **10**, 27, 28, 30, 42
color, **28**
comets, 8, 33
Copernicus, Nicolaus, 21
core, **28**, 29, 30

days, 15, 16, 18
Despina (moon), 33
diameter, 18
discovery, 11, 20–21, 22–25, 40
distance, 7
dwarf planets, 8, 14, 18, 20

Earth, 7, 8, 11, 13, 14, 15, 16, **17**, **19**, 22, **27**, 30, 31, 34, 36

Galileo, **25**
Galle, Johann, 20, 25
gas giants, **17**, **30**, **36**
gases, **10**, **15**, 17, 27, **28**, 29, 35
gravity, 15, 23, 34, 35, 37
Great Dark Spot, **31**

helium, 28
Herschel, Sir William, 21
hydrogen, 28

ice volcanoes, 35, 40

Jupiter, 8, 11, **14**, 17, **18**, **22**, **36**, 39, 40

Leverrier, Urbain, 11, **24**, 25
liquids, **10**, 17, 27, 29

Mars, 8, 11, 14, **18**, **22**
math, 24, 25

Mercury, 11, 14, **18**, **22**
methane gas, **28**
moons, 10, **14**, **19**, **32**, **33**, **35**, 37, 40, **42**

name, 11
Neptune/Triton Orbiter space probe, **42**
Nereid (moon), **34**

orbit, 14, 15, 16, 19, 20, 23, 27, **34**

Pluto, 8, 13, 14, **18–19**, 20, 41

rings, 10, **13**, **36**, **37**
Romans, **11**
rotation, **16**

Saturn, 8, 11, 14, 17, **19**, 21, **22**, **36**, 39, 40
size, **17**, 27
solar system, 8, 13, 14, **18–19**, 21, 22, 35, 37, 38, 41
space probes, **6**, **38**, **39–41**, **42**
storms, **30**, **31**
sun, **6**, 7, 8, 14, **15**, 16, **18–19**, 21, **23**, 27, 29, 41
surface, 10, **33**

telescopes, **12**, 13, 22, 24, **25**, 36
temperatures, 7, 29, 30, 35, 40
Tombaugh, Clyde, 20
Triton (moon), **32**, **33**, 34, **35**, 40, **42**

Uranus, 8, **9**, 14, 17, **18**, 21, **23**, 25, **36**, 39, 40

Venus, 11, 14, **19**, **22**
Voyager 2 space probe, **6**, 32, **38**, **39**, 40, **41**

weather, 27, **30**, **31**, 42
winds, 27, **30**, **31**

years, 15, 18

About the Author

Award-winning author Elaine Landau has a bachelor's degree from New York University and a master's degree in library and information science from Pratt Institute.

She has written more than 300 non-fiction books for children and young adults. Although Ms. Landau often writes on science topics, she especially likes writing about planets and space.

She lives in Miami, Florida, with her husband and son. The trio can often be spotted at the Miami Museum of Science and Space Transit Planetarium. You can visit Elaine Landau at her Web site: www.elainelandau.com.